This Thing Called Grief

This Thing Called Grief

New Understandings of Loss

Thomas M. Ellis

SYREN BOOK COMPANY
MINNEAPOLIS

Most Syren Books are available at special quantity discounts for bulk purchases for sales pro-
motions, premiums, fund-raising, and educational needs. For details, write

Syren Book Company, Special Sales Department
5120 Cedar Lake Road • Minneapolis, MN 55416

Published by
Syren Book Company • 5120 Cedar Lake Road • Minneapolis, MN 55416

Printed in the United States of America on acid-free paper

ISBN-13: 978-0-929636-64-1   ISBN-10: 0-929636-64-3
LCCN: 2006923497

Editing, design, & layout: E. B. Green Editorial, Saint Paul
Printing, binding: Syren Book Company, Minneapolis

To order additional copies of this book see the form
at the back of this book or go to www.itascabooks.com

Contents

In memory of those who have gone before us
and who continue to touch our lives with their stories,
especially
Donald Ellis
Stacy Wise Egan
and
all the beloved of the families I have been privileged to serve.

Preface

Tragedy and terror have become part of our American culture, and words like *grief* and *trauma* appear frequently in the media. Local television stations and newspapers have called upon me to help make sense of the realities of loss to the greater community. This book grows out of a demand to clarify and acknowledge what we experience following the death of someone we love.

I was born into a family that lived and worked in a small-town funeral home—yes, it was much like those depicted in the series *Six Feet Under* and the movie *My Girl*. Not uncommonly, Dad awakened us in the night as he was called to work or as he called on us for help at the scene of a death. I invariably knew the persons who died or some members of their families. Witnessing their pain was often tough for us, but it was what we did.

After one 3 a.m. death, I declared that I would never be a funeral director. I couldn't wait to grow up and move on. So, following a brief sojourn at school in another city, I decided to continue in the field of mortuary science and purchase the family business! My experience since then of being with others at times of death has been challenging and humbling.

My father suffered a brain tumor when I was in high school, which caused his total disability for the ten years preceding his death. My mother was the primary caregiver to this young man who could no longer talk or walk and who experienced periodic seizures. He became openly emotional—crying through my entire wedding, upon the announcement of my wife's pregnancy, and at the news of my purchasing his business. He never lived to see our daughters born, but Sarah has his Irish eyes and Kathryn, his zest for life. He loved beautiful girls.

You get the idea. Grief has played an active role in my life, which is why I have felt called to be with people in pain. Becoming a marriage and family therapist and director of the Center for Grief, Loss & Transition has given me an incredible opportunity to walk beside individuals and families who are experiencing terrible loss. I have learned that we are all changed by grief, whether we express it or not.

I believe that healing transitions can result in renewed lives for those in grief. I hope to help readers make sense of something that initially makes no sense at all. And so I share these ideas for healing from those who have been in great pain. The following stories are real. Names are used with permission or altered with identifying circumstances to maintain client privacy.

I gratefully acknowledge the many people who have touched my life not only with their stories but also with who they are as individuals. Working alongside others who have experienced great loss and healing grief is a privilege. The telling and retelling of your narratives is in itself healing.

Thanks to my colleagues who have passed through the doors of the Center for Grief, especially Walter Bera, Gayle Sherman-Crandell, Joanne Detwiler, Sandra Koch, and Sarah Logan. Yours is the work of angels amidst despair.

A special thank-you to Mary Anderson, Bruce and Jean Johnson, and Trudy Lapic for making the Center for Grief, Loss & Transition a viable nonprofit venture.

Most important, my wife, Marianne, and daughters, Sarah and Kathryn, have shared both sorrow and joy through years interwoven with loss and grief. I am grateful for your understanding and compassionate hearts.

—Thomas M. Ellis

Introduction

Grief is a crazy-making, complicated process. It is part of life's critical transitions, its times of loss. Losses include not only endings—dying and death—but also beginnings, which start with grief and mourning.

Grief has been described as a roller coaster of emotions. You might experience it as an engulfing wave, an ever-changing sea of experience, a place with nothing to protect you. Writer C. S. Lewis experienced grief as fear itself. Whatever you feel today, you learn that it will probably be different tomorrow.

Grief is not about clear, predictable stages or steps. Rather, it is a natural process of dynamic changes that will ebb and flow as they may. You experience grief across every dimension of your being—body, mind, and spirit. As author John Schneider says, "Grief is a natural process of discovering what was lost, what is left, and what is possible."

Ken, a father who witnessed the death of his two children in his car, described his grief as "walking through a tunnel in mud." Grief is relentless trudging, with unstable footing, in a dimly lit, strange place. Grief is a continuing personal process, a struggle to acknowledge the life-changing impact of loss. It affects the behavioral, cognitive, emotional, physical, and spiritual dimensions of the self.

Grief is depriving and painful in that it acknowledges that something has been taken away. You have lost someone and/or something. You are left with a painful void in your life. Grief is despairing, isolating, and overwhelming. Life suddenly changes, and its meaning is less clear than ever. Grief is disorganized and mischievous. It enjoys playing tricks on you and keeps you unbalanced.

There is a danger in discussing the life process of grief. You may be tricked into a place in which you gain a sense of final understanding. Beware the "grief expert." The only expert on grief is the person experiencing a particular loss at a particular time. You. Grief is so personally unique and changing that getting your mind and heart around it once and for all is impossible. Just when you reach a place of understanding, it changes again. Describing grief is like trying to hold water with your hands. You feel it, you see it, you smell it, and then it is gone. All that remains is a strange dampness.

Despite this dilemma, there is value in gathering as much information as possible, in pulling together some tools to help. This is what the following pages are about.

Someone or something is gone, and you are left with a broken heart. You feel a deep emptiness, a sense of deprivation. Grief and pain are changing you now, but they have the potential to transform your life in a healing way. Your capacity for courage is amazing. You have an inherent propensity for resilience.

You have unwillingly entered a new chapter in your life. But a nurturing environment, a few tools, and full permission for you to grieve will allow you to live again.

So what do you need to experience loss in a healthy way?

This Thing Called Grief

If we could read the secret history of our enemies,
We should find in each person's life
Sorrow and suffering enough to disarm all hostility.
—*Henry Wadsworth Longfellow*

1

Grieving Your Personal Losses

In 2004, Dick and Darliss's adult daughter Stacy died after a yearlong struggle with cancer. Their family had begun to grieve as Stacy first became ill.

That their daughter had a terrible disease and had to face the challenge of multiple therapies to combat it became too much for Dick and Darliss to bear. Confusion, isolation, frustration, anger, and overwhelming sadness quickly became their reality. Old behaviors and ways of being were no longer important. Work and volunteer commitments were no longer on their list of immediate priorities. A new demand for supporting one another shadowed social commitments—especially as their two young grandsons became aware of the impact of their mother's disease.

The struggle between a sense of hopefulness and the possibility of impending death was the first cognitive challenge for Dick and Darliss. How could they begin to acknowledge such a dilemma or even *try* to function in a meaningful way? Finding ways to express their constant struggle and to have the freedom to speak of it added to the already overwhelming demands on them.

This loving family sought support in the prayers of hundreds of friends. They brought their hope for a miracle to the forefront of their grief by gathering stones and writing the word *miracle* on each. They acknowledged the spiritual challenges in a healing service conducted at Stacy's church. The level of support received through these rituals allowed for an open expression of hope, sadness, and loss.

The ripple effects of Stacy's struggle for life began to plague the extended family as its members started their journey of ups and downs. Loss of vitality and zest for life challenged their world view. Individual roles had to shift as a team of supporters joined the ride.

Stacy's inability to mother as she had earlier became apparent. Others stepped in to fill the void, propelled by overwhelming emotion and an urgency to provide for the basic needs of a changed and changing family on a rest-of-their-lives journey of dashed hopes and dreams. There would be no more family photos with Stacy's beautiful smile—instead there would be pictures of a grieving family with affected expressions. Family vacations would continue but with a noticeable missing piece. Family experiences would no longer include the beloved Stacy.

Stacy's dying and death affected so many people, in so many ways. She left behind two young sons, a husband, her parents, two sisters, a brother, grandmother, and a multitude of friends and extended-family members. Her death will always impact those whose lives she touched—just as your loss will always affect you.

Grief enters your life in quiet, subtle ways or like a train running out of control. A chronic illness impacts your life, or perhaps your child has been diagnosed with a debilitating or terminal disease. You may be aware that grief was a part of your family's history before you arrived. Perhaps your grandparents experienced the Holocaust, or one of your parents struggled with a life-threatening illness. Abuse or neglect may be a part of your past. You have inherited grief stories that have become a part of who you are.

Throughout your life, you accumulate a multitude of losses. Living with a more recent loss may bring back old grief. You may have acknowledged some of these losses at the time, or you may have simply put them away. At any rate, grief is a cumulative creature that can grow larger over time. And if you try to hide from grief, it may cripple you.

You may not know all of the kinds of losses that may occur, especially when you lose a loved one. One way to understand loss and reaction to loss is to consider how losses may affect the five dimensions of self: behavioral, cognitive, emotional, physical, and spiritual.

The behavioral dimension pertains to your individual actions. The cognitive dimension affects how you perceive or know things. The emotional aspect affects consciousness of feelings, clearly distinguished from the cognitive, or thinking, dimension. Of course, the physical pertains to the losses and reactions of your body. Finally, the spiritual dimension pertains to the presence of spirit as distinguished from physical or worldly existence.

Gathering as much information as possible about your loss can reduce stress and allow you to become the expert on your grief. Being able to name what you have lost, as well as the ripple effects created by your loss, will help you begin your personal process of grieving.

Giving your grief the time it demands can help you to begin a healing process. Acknowledging what has been lost can provide new insights into how your life has been affected by your loss. The following lists may help you to discover the ripple effects of your loss or accumulated losses, whether they are due to death, divorce, or other life transitions. Remember that there may be other undiscovered or ambiguous losses of which you are not yet fully aware.

Behavioral Losses
(individual actions)

- Self-expression
- Dependence
- Job
- Vocation
- Sexual function
- Role(s)
- Independence
- Profession
- Career
- Social activity
- Income

Cognitive Losses
(how you perceive or know things)

- Safety
- Trust
- Dream(s)
- Body image
- Self-esteem
- Security
- Sense of sexuality
- Plans for the future
- Lifestyle
- Memory
- Mental sharpness
- Youth

You may find it helpful to check the items in these lists that speak to your losses personally or to the losses of your family. Some people find it useful to differentiate between losses experienced as a child and losses experienced as an adult. This exercise may also bring awareness

Emotional Losses
(consciousness of how you feel)

- Mother
- Family
- Relationship(s)
- Sibling
- Infant
- Grandchild
- Childhood
- Friend
- Grandparent
- Father
- Marriage
- Partner
- Child
- Pregnancy
- Relative
- Home
- Possessions
- Pet

Physical Losses
(how your body feels and reacts)
- Fertility
- Health
- Hair
- Sight
- Body part
- Mobility
- Intimacy

of losses that are not on the list. Again, being able to name what you have lost will help you to develop a deeper understanding of why you feel the way you do. Expressing your thoughts and feelings with trusted others and/or with written words will release some of your despair.

Some individuals experience fear or anxiety at the mere idea of focusing on their own loss and grief: What good can come from acknowledging something sad? What if I start to cry and cannot stop? Could I have a breakdown if I pay too close attention to my grief? Will I create more sadness or despair by facing my losses?

Spiritual Losses
(aspects of the spirit)

- Friendship
- Community
- Freedom
- Self-worth
- Faith
- Religion
- Self
- Hope
- Relationship with God
- Supportive environment
- Prayer life
- Desire to worship

These common concerns potentially postpone the grief work necessary for beginning to heal. Remember that exploring your personal-loss history will not create new losses. It will give you the permission to acknowledge what has happened to you.

You can begin to make some sense of your life by bringing a new awareness of your losses to your attempt to understand your grief. Such exploration of your loss is an essential part of grief therapy, one with which you can create a new level of self-awareness.

Many grief experiences, especially those complicated by a traumatic death, don't offer the option of initial denial or acceptance. The images, thoughts, and feelings related to loss are too overwhelming to avoid.

Ken and Lorrie, one couple experiencing such a loss, entered my office a few months after the death of their two youngest children. They had been a family of five—Mike almost seven, Matt turning five, and Megan just nine months. The couple had recently decided that, with three beautiful children, their family was complete. They were on a track for success in their life ahead. On the evening before the accident the family had celebrated Matt's fifth birthday.

The next afternoon, Ken was ill and home from work. He decided to ride along with Lorrie, Matt, and Megan to pick up Mike at school, just a few blocks from their new home. On the way back from school to their home, a large, commercial dump truck rear-ended their van.

Both Ken and Lorrie remember being trapped in their vehicle, not fully comprehending the accident. They could see their youngest children, Matt and Megan, but they could not reach them. They could do nothing but watch and wait until help arrived.

Ambulances rushed them to the closest emergency hospital. Ken was dazed, Lorrie and Mike had major injuries, and Matt and Megan were killed instantly. Lorrie had several broken bones in her back and was hospitalized for ten days. Ken had broken ribs. Their son Mike sustained serious head injuries and numerous broken bones. He was in a coma, in Intensive Care. Ken later described his feeling of watching a person who looked like himself, walking through the halls of the hospital between Mike in Intensive Care and Lorrie in her room.

Ken and Lorrie were left to deal with the pain every parent fears. Two of their children were dead, and the other was barely holding on to life. What had begun as a wonderfully hopeful day had suddenly become a terrible nightmare. They were forced down a road they did not choose. Their journey in grief had just begun.

After years of family therapy, Ken and Lorrie are still amazed at how much time they spent working through their trauma, their relationship, and their changed family circumstances. They had had no understanding that two people, as close as they felt to each other, could experience such different feelings at different times. At first, they were aware of their shared loss but not of their own, individual reactions. The stress on their relationship and the challenges to their healthy communication threw them for a loop.

Ken and Lorrie needed to explore all the things they had lost individually and together. They worked to recognize the secondary losses created by their children's deaths, which gradually became more visible. They explored the loss of their value system, companionship, careers, and the loss of their individual selves.

This is what is meant by a life-changing event. Virtually everything changed for Ken and Lorrie—from life before the loss to life after the loss. Exploring the multitude of their loss helped them to create a new awareness of their grief and a renewed appreciation for each other's losses. They became the experts on their own personal grief and the witnesses to each other's pain. Later, Lorrie wrote the following verses.

My Life

My life before the accident
Was a beautiful dream come true.
I met your dad, got married,
And had all three of you.

My life before the accident
Was filled with joy each day.
I had the life I longed for
And thought it was here to stay.

My life after the accident
Is full of memories to carry me through
Until the day our family
Is reunited with both of you.

With Hope

This is not at all
How we thought it was supposed to be.
We had so many plans for you.
We had so many dreams.
And now you've gone away
And left us with the memories of your smile.
And nothing we can say
And nothing we can do
Can take away the pain, the pain of losing you, but
We can cry with hope, we can say goodbye with hope
'Cause we know our goodbye is not the end.
And we can grieve with hope 'cause we believe with hope,
There's a place where we'll see your face again . . .

—*Steven Curtis Chapman*

2

Responses to Your Grief

I met Katy at an educational workshop—"Grief through the Eyes of a Child"—designed to bring a specific awareness and helping tools to educators.

Here she was, the young mother of two, desperately looking for help and for ideas about how to comfort her grieving children. She had found her way to this setting, drawn by the topic but clearly in need of individual and family therapy focusing on the death of her husband. Katy was openly expressive about her situation and the caring group quickly embraced her. The workshop had attracted mostly teachers and social workers, who immediately understood the situation. We moved through the agenda at hand, and Katy later contacted me for individual and family therapy.

Katy had been home with her family when her son came running into the house to report that Dad had fallen on the driveway. That afternoon changed their family forever. Dan had died immediately, and Katy found herself on a path she feared more than anything. How could she live without her childhood sweetheart, the one she had depended on for so many things?

Katy's initial reactions of shock, disbelief, and fear were complicated by the traumatic and sudden way in which Dan had died. She was reeling from flashbacks of what they all had witnessed at their home and from trying to pay attention to the needs of her children. These quickly launched her into a place of despair and overwhelming grief. She reported extreme fatigue, memory loss, preoccupation with her husband's death, a decreased level of functioning, sadness, anxiety, blunted emotions, and excessive crying, to name only a few.

Katy acknowledged multiple grief reactions on a checklist provided to new clients entering therapy, much like the ones in this chapter. She was experiencing frequent headaches, unexplained aches and pains, slowed movements, difficulty breathing, restlessness, lack of concentration, changes in her relationships, lowered self-esteem, decreased pleasure, anger, guilt, and mood swings. She had a short fuse. Her checklist was a snapshot of her personal grief responses, all normal but terribly overwhelming.

How do we begin to understand the complicated, misunderstood experience of grief? I like to begin conferences by asking the participants whether they know anything about the "stages" of grief. There are usually a few professionals who begin by sharing the words of Elisabeth Kübler-Ross—shock, denial, anger, and so forth. Soon it becomes clear that these old understandings, which give a false sense that grief can be organized in simple, linear steps, are difficult to shed.

Kübler-Ross's work was a breakthrough for beginning to understand the dying, not the grieving, process. Nevertheless, her understandings have enabled our culture to begin to put words to these life experiences and given us permission to discuss the possibilities. Such continuing dialogue is critical both for those who are grieving and for those (professionals) who wish to help. We must recognize various grief experiences and the reactions that follow.

So—if grief is not about clear, predictable stages—how do you make sense of it? This is one of the classic tricks of grief—you need to make sense of your life experience, yet grief makes no sense at all. Just when you think you have a handle on it, something changes. You are confused and surprised by how grief plays with you. You take one step forward and three steps back. Just when the light of day begins to appear, you find yourself back in the darkness of despair.

The clarity that can arise from your paying attention to these reactions will give you understanding of how dynamic and nonlinear this thing called grief is. It's like watching an eagle fly over the shores of Lake Superior. It seems to hang so high in the air and its flight appears effortless. Then something triggers its attention, and the pattern quickly changes. There may be a plunge to the cold, dark waters below. Or there may be a series of gentle swoops, up and down over the water—so graceful, so powerful.

Grief is a naturally occurring process of loss, experienced through every dimension of your being. You suddenly begin to talk about how everything has changed. You switch the lens through which you view the world. What was once important is important no longer. What was once enjoyable is now mundane. You understand life in terms of "before the loss" and "after the loss." You don't know your reflection: "Where is the old me, and what have they done to me?"

Grief is best understood as an open, circular loop from which you feel you cannot escape. You have lost someone or something, and you are lost in a maze. You may protest or try to ignore what is happening. You search for any distraction—a great way to deny your new, overwhelming feelings and reactions.

One indication of this coping mechanism is a tendency to throw yourself into your work. Keeping busy so as to have limited idle time may become your preferred way of being. Being at home with the reminders of what you have lost may be too much to bear. Increased interest and indulgence in travel and other hobbies may fill your days. Such distractions ease the first, painful responses to loss, but they do not replace or rid you of the thoughts and feelings that are part of grief.

You may find yourself in a place of despair, not knowing which way to turn, not knowing even how to breathe fully. You question everything you have ever believed in. You are not the only one to respond to loss in this way. After the death of his beloved wife, C. S. Lewis questioned everything he had ever written. He felt physically different from how he felt before she died. Lewis wrote in 1961:

> No one ever told me that grief felt so like fear. I am not afraid, but the sensation is like being afraid. The same fluttering in the stomach, the same restlessness, the yawning. I keep on swallowing. At other times it

feels like being mildly drunk, or concussed. There is a sort of invisible blanket between the world and me. I find it hard to take in what anyone says. Or perhaps, hard to want to take it in. It is so uninteresting. Yet I want the others to be about me. I dread the moments when the house is empty. If only they would talk to one another and not to me.

Ask yourself, "What does my grief look like?" To gain a deeper understanding of the nature of grief, you must observe it in all its vagaries. How do you experience life after your loss? Is anything the same? What is different? Taking time to look at what others have experienced as common grief reactions can help normalize your response, validate what you are living with, and help you know that you are not alone.

On the following pages are some common responses to loss. Have you experienced these responses or others? Know that all are "normal" reactions to loss. The long list can help explain why you feel the way you feel. But you must also be aware of signs that suggest more complicated reactions. Grieving becomes more complicated when the pain of your loss is extreme and it becomes too large to embrace. You may have been dealt more than you alone (or anyone alone) can handle.

Behavioral Reactions

- Detachment from family and friends
- Changes in interests and activities
- Isolation
- Decreased socialization
- Changes in sexual activity
- Changes in relationships
- Changes in work productivity
- Loss of pleasure
- Short fuse
- Loneliness
- Change in activity level

Grief can quickly become depression, a distortion of reality, or a battle of avoidance. This twist in the process may occur for various reasons. A traumatic death from homicide, suicide, or an accident, for instance, holds the potential to create a shift in your reality and your sense of safety in the world. Unexpected loss can jolt you from the very sense of who you are. The death of a child takes away your sense of future as you envisioned it.

Cognitive Reactions

- Lack of concentration
- Difficulty in making decisions
- Preoccupation with your loss
- Being distracted
- Decreased attention span
- Short-term memory loss
- Confusion
- Lowered self-esteem
- Worry
- Feeling overwhelmed

If you have experienced and listed multiple losses, your list may prompt your first realization that there is just too much for you to deal with. Your cup overflows with pain and fear. Intense feelings of revenge or blame shade the common ways of coping with grief. Your sadness may turn to depression or detachment from those around you.

Complicated loss may complicate your grief. You may become stuck in taking in your terrible reality. The myriad losses resulting from a death or other loss are devastating and too painful to acknowledge.

Emotional Reactions

- Mood swings
- Fear
- Panic attacks
- Sadness
- Numbness
- Anger
- Anxiety
- Shock
- Disbelief
- Guilt
- Blunted emotions
- Excessive crying
- Shame

Grief may interfere with your ability to function; guilt and anger may become overwhelming. Withdrawal from others, thoughts of hurting yourself or someone else, and addictive behaviors may become part of your new identity. Differentiating fantasy and reality may become a challenge. A lack of energy and will to live may become familiar.

Physical Reactions

- Difficulty falling asleep/nightmares
- Difficulty staying asleep
- Early-morning wakening
- Increase in appetite
- Decrease in appetite
- Change in weight
- Nausea
- Indigestion
- Headaches
- Stomachaches
- Fatigue
- Lack of energy
- Unexplained aches and pains
- Lump in your throat
- Slowed movement
- Tightness in your chest
- Frequent colds or flu
- Difficulty breathing
- Restlessness

Spiritual Reactions

- Change in belief system
- Change in values
- Sense of hopelessness
- Change in support system
- Questioning faith
- Questioning religious affiliation
- Disconnection from self
- Change in relationship with God
- Shift in prayer life
- Change in desire to worship
- Shift in priorities

Nancy's grief (and her children's) initially was complicated in that her husband disappeared—he was missing. The family did not know whether he was alive or dead. Did he have an accident? Had he been kidnapped? Was he the victim of a murder? Or suicide? The family didn't know and so held out for a hopeful ending to their story.

Two weeks after the family reported him missing, he was found, beaten to death. The family had been directly involved in the search, and at one time its members were close to the site where he was murdered. The traumatic nature of his death, the continuing investigations, the pending trials further clouded the family's experience with grief.

The necessary investigation and legal proceedings, soon a central part of Nancy's and her children's lives, multiplied their victimization. Individuals in the family experienced disparate grief responses at different levels, at different times.

Nancy had no trouble sleeping. She experienced great fatigue and a demand for more sleep. Her youngest child demonstrated much different physical reactions. He experienced disturbed sleep patterns, nightmares, and extreme feelings of fear and anxiety.

Nancy felt a need for all the information she could gather about how her husband had died, but her children wished not to know any of the details of their father's death. Their separate lives and once-complete family changed forever.

Nancy's losses forced her into a life she did not want. With no energy to lift even herself, she now had to run various family businesses and raise two children by herself. Her losses were a challenge across every dimension. She experienced overwhelming sadness, anger, and disbelief about her husband's death. She was challenged by a lack of concentration and a lack of the ability to make decisions. Her grief journey required great patience and multiple layers of support.

To begin its healing, grief requires an honest understanding of the responses to and validation of a new reality—many new realities. You need permission to tell your story without being judged or ridiculed. Having access to someone who will listen to your difficult story without putting a time frame on the experience is essential. You cannot journey through this process in isolation. You need individuals who understand your experience. And you may need a professional with competence in grief-and-trauma therapy to help you bear what no one can bear alone.

No one can tell you how to grieve or for how long. But what is normal? Perhaps the best understanding is that what you are experiencing now is where you now need to be on your journey. Explore the physical and emotional responses listed previously in an intentional way. Don't minimize or ignore the power of grief.

Grief is about the completeness of the circle of life and death. Entrances and exits—birth, life, and death—are a large part of the human experience. Grief is a reality of the life process, something everyone experiences at one time or another, to one degree or another.

Falling Apart

I seem to be falling apart
My attention span can be measured in seconds
My patience in minutes
I cry at the drop of a hat
I forget things constantly
The morning toast burns daily
I forget to sign the checks
Half of everything in the house is misplaced
Feelings of anxiety and restlessness are my constant
    companions
Rainy days seem extra dreary
Sunny days seem an outrage
Other people's pain and frustration seem insignificant
Laughing, happy people seem out of place in my
    world
It has become routine to feel half crazy
I am normal I am told
I am a newly grieving person.

—Eloise Cole

Acts of Helplessness

Here are the miracle signs you want:
That you cry through the night and get up at dawn,
Asking, that in the absence of what you ask for your day
    gets dark,
Your neck thin as a spindle, that what you give away, is all
    you own,
That you sacrifice belongings, sleep, health, your head,
That you often sit down in a fire like aloes wood,
And often go out to meet a blade like a battered helmet.
When acts of helplessness become habitual, those are
    signs.
But you run back and forth listening for unusual events,
Peering into the faces of travelers.
"Why are you looking at me like a madman?"
I have lost a friend. Please forgive me.
Searching like that does not fail.
There will come a rider who holds you close.
You faint and gibber. The uninitiated say, "He's faking."
How could they know?
Water washes over a beached fish, the water of those signs
    I just mentioned.
Excuse my wandering.
How can one be orderly with this?
It's like counting leaves in a garden, along with the song
    notes of partridges, and crows,
Sometimes organization and computation become absurd.

                                                    —*Rumi*

3

Dispelling the Myths That Bind

Lucy came to the Center for Grief, Loss & Transition upon the recommendation of a concerned friend. She explained how her beloved husband had been killed in a plane crash and how her life had become empty. This charming, intelligent, young widow was overwhelmed by her loss, yet she wondered whether she really needed to talk about it. She consistently apologized for being a burden. And she watched the clock, so as not to trouble me for any more time than was absolutely necessary. Perhaps like you, she wasn't sure she needed a therapist.

The oppressive ideas placed upon you by your culture may appear to contain your traumatic, complicated grief. You wonder whether it is all right to express your feelings. Or, if you do express your emotions, will you appear to be weak or perceived not to be doing so well? Comparing your reactions to loss with those of others, or making judgments as to what grief must look like, challenges the healing process. Such thought processes may block what could be the natural, open expression of feelings. If so, the potential for isolation increases. Lucy was challenged by such misunderstandings of her grief experience.

Death, loss, and grief are realities of life. But few of us feel comfortable openly conversing about these critical life experiences. Talking about such realities is taboo in our society, and many preconceptions shape basic understandings of how the grief process should work. Many generations of families, cultural traditions, religious and spiritual beliefs, gender expectations, literature, media interpretations, and other influences have given birth to the perceptions we share.

You almost certainly approach the grieving process with some preconceived notions that may inhibit your healing process. Understanding what you bring to your grief and what may get in the way of your healing may be helpful. Use the following list to help you discover what grief might mean to you and to your family:

Reconceptions of Common Preconceived Ideas

- Grief is not about stages you go through and ultimately graduate from. Rather it is a dynamic process of ups and downs, fluctuating with painful and peaceful moments, hours, days, and weeks.

- Grief is not something you get over. Instead it is an experience that you must go through directly, taking in all of the thoughts, feelings, and behaviors that you encounter along the way.

- Grief is not time-limited, nor does time heal all wounds. A common misconception is that you grieve for one year and on the anniversary of the loss you will return to "normal." This concept promotes a sense of failure and concern. In reality, grief demands the time it needs. Healing requires active participation in grieving.

- Everyone does not experience grief in the same manner everyone else does. Grief is unique to each individual and experience. Give yourself permission to be free of others' expectations, and grant that freedom to others to explore and heal in ways that are real to them. Comparing and judging the losses and grieving processes of others is divisive, unproductive.

- Grief cannot be avoided. It waits for you and eventually demands your attention. Approaching grief is often scary, and you may fear that it will upset you and others around you. But the pain is already there, and nothing can make it worse. Denial will not relieve the present anxiety— expression will. The open expression of grief is a challenge in our modern society.

- Children and adults do not experience or express grief in the same ways. Children tend to grieve in small doses, followed by periods of play and distraction. They do not always have the information and words to express themselves. But yes, they are grieving.

- Grief may isolate you from family and friends. Keeping it private and personal doesn't make it go away.

- At times, people who are grieving may feel like having fun or laughing. You may need this. Fear of being judged or of piling on more guilt may prevent this. It's okay to take breaks from the exhausting work of grief.

Once in a great while I have the privilege of facilitating a men's grief group, typically made up of previous individual clients. They come from all walks of life—grief has no barriers. Their stories are diverse, but their experiences are relevant to all participants. In one fascinating group were individuals who had undergone multiple losses, including children, spouses, jobs, and loss to suicide. I was initially tentative as to how its members would receive a gentleman who was in a life transition because of unemployment. I was concerned about how he might feel in a room full of people who had recently experienced the death of a significant other.

Would his loss be judged in comparison to theirs? Could the members of the group go beyond their culturally influenced ideas about the dynamics of grief? Would they be challenged by the different time frames of the various losses? Some of these men were working through losses from years ago, while others experienced acute grief responses from current losses.

Still, I knew these men and the level of pain and compassion they held together. The fact that they were willing to participate in a group experience at all spoke volumes. Each carried a terrible burden in his experience of life, and each had the courage and compassion to bring it forward. My hope was that they could be true to their grief, sharing openly the thoughts and feelings weighing on their minds and hearts.

The group was receptive and supportive of every man and every story. Each man was able to listen to similar and differing experiences with an open heart and understanding mind. Judgmental words seldom interfered with the high level of compassionate listening. There were times when the loss of work and the inability to support a family became the focus.

What a testimony to the fact that grief is not limited by what is lost and how much time has passed! These men clearly embraced each other's pain in their willingness to become vulnerable by sharing their stories. This opened up a rare and healing forum that changed us all. The losses of children, spouses, and livelihood transcended any preconceived notions that could enter this sacred gathering.

Examining the myths or misunderstandings you harbor can help you to understand your personal ways of grieving. This new level of awareness can give you the permission you need to step out of your old ways of being and bring new meaning to this difficult process. You can begin to see yourself in new ways and to develop a foundation for understanding those around you.

Everyone comes to grief with different expectations, philosophies, and experience. Validating your own losses and acknowledging that all grief experiences are unique can help you to realize the complexities of bereavement—and to know what the heart of grief is about.

I am being driven forward into an unknown land.
The pass grows steeper, the air colder and sharper.
A wind from my unknown goal stirs the strings of
　　expectation.
Still the question: Shall I ever get there?
There where life resounds, a clear pure note in the
　　silence . . .

—Dag Hammarskjöld

Geese

Fact 1: As each bird flaps its wings, it creates uplift for the birds following it. By flying in a V-formation, the whole flock achieves a 71 percent greater flying range than if the bird flew alone.

Fact 2: Whenever a goose falls out of formation, it suddenly feels the drag and resistance of trying to fly alone and quickly gets back into formation to take advantage of the lifting power of the bird immediately in front.

Fact 3: When the lead goose gets tired, it rotates back into the formation, and another goose flies at the point position.

Fact 4: The geese in formation honk from behind to encourage those in front to keep up their speed.

Fact 5: When a goose becomes sick, is wounded, or shot down, two geese drop out of formation and follow it down to help and protect it. They stay with it until it is able to fly again or dies. Then they launch out on their own with another formation to catch up with the flock.

—*Tova Green and Peter Woodrow*

4

Grieving as a Family

In my experience, both professional and personal, grieving families experience life-changing transitions. The death of a loved one forever changes them. My father died in 1986, following ten years of disability as a result of his brain tumor. My family's transition began with his illness, yet its impact was not truly felt until his death.

My father's death marked the beginning of a new chaos—one without his leadership, support, and understanding. An integral piece of the family was missing. Lifestyles, family roles, and support systems changed. Some of us became detached from my father and the family, while others felt a connection to him and other members of the group. The telling and retelling of our stories was limited, and we sought no professional support.

As our experience together continues, the relationships ebb and flow. My personal connection with my father grows as I continue to grow. He remains a vital part of my life both in memory and through a strong sense of his presence. I reflect upon what his thoughts and words would be in a given life situation. I ask questions about how he would respond to what I am doing, what he feels towards my family, and why things turn out a certain way. He answers. I believe this connection enables me to be who I am and supports my relationships with others. We grieve because we have loved, and through love we can be healed.

Grieving is a family affair. You don't experience it in isolation. The balance of the family system is disrupted. A new and changed family develops. Throughout your grief experience you will notice many ways that you and your family are changing. You have lost an important part of who you were and many other things as a result of that loss. The once-familiar structure and patterns of family interaction are changed.

Ordinary understanding is not enough to comprehend the loss and sorrow following the death of a family member. The family's ordinary fabric of being and expectation is brutally torn. Death has interrupted and shocked your world, creating a peculiar wrongness and great intensity of feeling.

In all types of loss, the severity of response depends upon the degree to which the individual or family reality system has been attacked. This sense of reality is based on your personal history as an individual, in a family, community, and society. It dictates how you relate to others in your world. When a parent dies, a large part of a child's reality system changes forever. Part of the past has died. What was once safe and nurturing is no longer so.

Many environmental factors, including the quality of relationship before the death and the psychological continuity of the child's surviving environment, also influence the grief response. Spiritual beliefs, supportive relationships, a strong sense of self, and the availability of someone to listen to the story are just a few of the factors that may contribute to or detract from a balanced recovery.

Paying attention to what has changed throughout your family is an integral piece of working through grief in a healthy way. Ripple effects of loss may include loss of lifestyle, freedom, dreams, hopes, purpose, and roles, to name only a few. These ideas were listed earlier (see chapter 1). Acknowledge the changes that affect you.

What roles did your loved one fulfill? If he was responsible for organizing the family holidays and traditions, for instance, who will continue that task? Perhaps she was in charge of the fun in your home—who will now take this on? If the loved one was responsible for emotions, how will this affect your future? What are these missing pieces for your family? You may discover that no one will reclaim some of the roles, which adds another degree of change for each family member.

Family grieving may allow individual family members to shift roles and relationships to compensate for their loss. Family ties may strengthen as a result of identifying what has changed. You may also begin to identify the member who allows open expressions of grief, the one who ignores grief, and the ones who mask it. When mourning becomes individual and private, healthy family growth diminishes. But if you are able to integrate your loss, you will transform your life. This gives meaning to your loss and helps you to maintain connection. The family that grieves together restores the ability to love, an ability often impaired by loss. Sharing grief and pain can help prevent splitting and deterioration of your family.

Following the unexpected death of his young wife and the mother of his children, Joe described how, overnight, he had become a single parent. He had always admired and wondered how anyone could fill the role of two parents. And here he was, not feeling admirable at all. His two surviving children began to notice that Dad spent more time with them. And he was no longer so busy or stressed as he used to be. This father had great anxiety about trying to fill the shoes of his wife, and he accepted that he could not do it. Not only had he lost his companion, best friend, and happily married life, but also the mother of his children. Joe grieved for himself, his children, and mostly for what his wife was missing: "It all seems so wrong! She should be here with us."

The members of this changed family surrounded themselves with personal and professional support. Joe engaged in social events with other families to gain support for himself and especially for his children. Individual therapy for the members of his family was crucial to their finding insight and making a plan for a hopeful future. They also benefited from family therapy sessions, which allowed some difficult conversations to take place.

This work enabled them to discuss what had happened to their family and to air the worries they had for each other. Once they addressed their individual and family needs, each participated in a grief support group. There is great value in the opportunity to share with others who have similar losses. It is hard to comprehend that someone else may be experiencing the same feelings after a loss like your own.

The support that Joe's family received did not replace the losses, but it did allow all of the family members to function to the best of their abilities. Joe became an exceptional single parent. He quickly realized the need for more nurturing time with his children. And he is intentional in providing what was important to his wife in being a good parent. The family has created an environment in which its members cherish their memories through thoughtful and loving conversation. The mother continues to impact her family through the couple's previous openness and established priorities for a healthy family: "She would be so proud of our kids and thrilled with the transformations we continue to work on!"

The telling and retelling of the family story has been a vital piece of its walk. The father, the children, and their extended family find it helpful to know that not everyone is going to be in the same place at the same time in the grief process. Each member likely will undertake various tasks of grief at a different rate and in his or her own way. Understanding other members' positions and exploring each other's feelings help to restore equilibrium to the family. The idea that because you are family you should grieve in the same way is a classic trickster effect of loss.

Your ways of grieving are also directly impacted by your family of origin. Whether you like it or not, you are where you've come from. Generations of characters have impacted your life. Exploring your experience of grief in comparison to your parents' and their parents' expression of feelings and emotions around loss is important work.

We learn from those who have come before us, and we all have a natural tendency to promote our own pasts. Layered upon these assumptions is the human tendency to repeat behaviors, even ones that don't work in our favor. We try harder and harder until we discover (maybe) that our attempts are not helping us to attain our goals. Ask yourself, "How is this working for me?"

Considering the culture you were raised in, the nationalities that influence you, and the subtle rules you've inherited may bring further insight into your grieving. Your religious background (or lack of one) and spiritual beliefs play a big role in shaping your grief process. Some of these personal influences may be of comfort, while others may become barriers to your healing.

If you identify that you are a family of few words and many inhibitions around expressing thoughts and feelings, grieving in a healthy way may be a challenge. Such a challenge may require an outside-of-the-family voice—a helpful friend, member of the clergy, or a professional in grief and family therapy. Identifying the challenge and using available support will launch your grieving family onto a path of healing growth.

Time Is Standing Still for Me

Time is standing still for me
Looking back at what used to be
Thoughts of them whirling in my head
Looking forward with such dread

Can I move on without letting go?
Sometimes I can't see how so
Are memories enough to carry me
    through?
Oh how desperately I miss you

What can the future hold for me?
Wishing it would always be
The family that we were before
The family that we are no more

Time is standing still for me
Imagining how my new life could be
Holding you both within my heart
We will truly never be apart

—Mom

Some Things That Fly There Be

Some things that fly there be
Birds, hours, the bumblebees
Of these things no elegy
Some things that stay there be
Grief, hills, eternity
Nor this behooves me
There are that resting, rise
Can I expound the skies?
How still the riddle lies . . .

—*Emily Dickinson*

5

Your Changed World

The words of Emily Dickinson at left embrace the overwhelming reality of Ken and Lorrie's losses upon the one-year anniversary of the accidental death of their two children. During their course of therapy, they realized that friends and family had made a shift in their grief and perceived sense of support. Frustration and sadness pushed Ken and Lorrie's need to communicate their experiences to those they loved. A result of this realization was the following letter, discussed in therapy as a means to express their continuing grief experience:

> Dear Family and Friends,
>   It has been 14 months since we lost Matt and Megan. Some people say that after the one-year mark,

things get easier. They do not. We are able to go about our daily routine, take care of Michael, and look somewhat put together. However, the pain is as hurtful as the day it all happened.

There are times we can put our pain aside and laugh with others. And sometimes we can even look into the future and feel hopeful. Other times, it is a struggle to get out of bed. It is still very necessary for the three of us to cry often.

It is helpful for us to know our children will not be forgotten. We need to talk about them, speak their names, remembering what each of them did or said while they were here. Please do not be afraid to talk to us. Please do not worry about making us cry. Our sadness is always on the surface. Allowing us to talk and cry is giving us the best gift.

We will never quite be the same people we were before. How could we be? Life looks different to us now. Life has new meaning. We don't expect anyone to understand what it feels like for us. Grief is a vicious, demanding, necessary process.

Please don't rush us through—it doesn't work that way. We ask that you be willing to listen. We don't expect advice or for you to make things better.

This story, indicating the reality of support that most grieving individuals receive, is all too common. There seem to be limits to the time allowed for grief. And there is pressure to "get on with life." Your family's view of the world changes dramatically, yet the rest of the old world moves on. You may have expectations of how family and friends will react to your loss, of how they will create a sense of support.

The truth is, breakdown of this supportive system may further complicate the already demanding process of your grief. Not only have you experienced the loss of loved ones, but now the people you thought would be helpful are not available to sit with you in your pain.

"No one understands what I am experiencing."

"I have changed so much; my friends seem to be avoiding me."

"My family tells me to move on with the rest of my life."

"I feel so alone in my grief."

These are just a few of the statements of active grievers. Change is inevitable, and change in grief is everywhere. If you have struggled with adjusting to change in the past, you must pay attention to the challenge before you. You must also pay attention to any inclination to worry about what others may think of you. People may judge you and even criticize your grieving.

Recently I overheard a group of women talking about funerals. One participant shared with the others how the women at her church talk about grieving families. This idea grabbed my attention and began to frustrate me. The individual went on to share her observations about funerals for which she had recently volunteered. She seemed most concerned about families predicting inaccurately the number of people who would attend a funeral luncheon. And she began to judge past services. She reminded me of how powerful the spoken word can be.

Sometimes it is easy for people to focus on trivial concerns in the face of loss. They can be insensitive—without realizing what they say or how it may impact others. We must pay attention to the reality of others and think before we speak. If you are in grief, this is a time to be near those who understand with tenderness and caring acts. Grief is hard, exhausting work. Focusing on what is really important will facilitate your transition into a changed world.

Another thing likely to change is your address book. The friends you predicted would hang in there are often nowhere to be found, but a new support system may spring forth. (Perhaps this is why my mother makes entries in her address book in pencil.) Your expectations of others may increase, with resulting disappointment and further frustration. Discovering who makes up your support system and how it seems to change can minimize your feelings of rejection or sense of being judged.

Changes in spirituality may be another area of challenge. Loss and grief may shake the foundation of your belief system. You may begin to question old beliefs, some you held even as a child. It is perfectly normal to wonder where God is in all of this turmoil. You may find this a time of great introspection and searching for spiritual guidance. Is it okay to question God's plan? Is it okay to blame God? Is there a life or a heaven after death? Is life supposed to be fair? Can I just continue to give it all to God?

Rabbi Harold Kushner has written many helpful books, including *When Bad Things Happen to Good People,* on this topic. Note that his title is not why bad things happen, but when. Bad things do happen, and asking for spiritual direction from someone you know and trust may be crucial to a healthy grieving process. Some members of the clergy devote their ministry to working with individuals who are questioning their faith and perhaps entering a new level of spirituality. Intentionally seeking spiritual support and guidance may provide you a critical safety net on your path of change.

Other changes may develop in your responses to the ever-changing grief process. The list of grief reactions addressed in chapter 2 may begin to shift for you and your family. There may be a time of softening in which a new sense of healing prevails—a cognitive shift in the new you. You may begin to transform and incorporate emotional sadness into newfound joys. Such are the moments in which to celebrate change. Know that these times may be fleeting. You may be reminded of the undulating quality of grief with its dynamic ups and downs. Glimmers of hope and happiness may be few and far between, but acknowledging these moments of respite may help to balance your times of despair.

Changes in relationships may occur or become clearer as you move through your grief. Relationships are complicated by the inherent differences between men and women. Grief doesn't discriminate between gender and culture, but men and women tend to do the work of grief in different ways. Our great society has placed clear expectations and requirements upon men and women.

Young men quickly learn to express themselves in "appropriate" behavior through statements like "Stand up and take it like a man," or "It's your responsibility—you're the man of the house," and "That's a man's job." They also learn that men usually communicate with one another in a side-by-side, not a face-to-face manner—riding in a car, walking down the street, or during a game of golf. This approach is most comfortable for most men.

Women typically enjoy sitting around a table or in a comfortable room, openly sharing personal thoughts and concerns. Their support system is more readily available. Men usually deny themselves and each other this level of support, looking to handle their stresses and loss issues alone. Thus most support groups are made up of women.

Of course, there are exceptions—the "men's grief group" mentioned earlier, for one. The individuals there accepted one another and allowed for a sharing of thoughts and feelings not often experienced by men. But men typically try to appear to be in control of life's demands and generally submit to societal demands that they:

- remain emotionally and physically strong
- always be rational
- refrain from crying and publicly mourning
- remain self-sufficient, without asking for support or affection
- remain as non-expressive as possible
- provide, don't nurture
- fix it, don't just accept it
- shake hands, don't hug

While the above expectations may appear to be generalizations, they continue to hold power over men in pain.

What men need to hear instead is that tears are a gift towards healing. Historically, you have been robbed of this important gift. Approaching the subject of cultural expectations of how men must grieve can give you permission to share your thoughts in a more meaningful and supportive way. Realizing that grief can be a constructive, healing process, shared with others, may inspire you to be intentional about how you fully grieve. Simply knowing that a positive chemical reaction occurs when you cry is important. Crying rids your body of poisons and prompts your brain to release endorphins that help your whole system relax and make you feel better.

The message here is that men can be strong and gentle, feeling and tough, all at the same time. The myth about crying must be reworked—it takes a strong man to be able to cry. It's no coincidence that men die seven years younger than women and have a 10 percent lower life expectancy. Gender differences in nursing home populations (women live longer) also speak to the issue.

What you need in grief is affiliation, loyalty, and intimacy. Do those words describe your personal relationships? Do you deal with life's difficulties alone or with others? What can you do to lessen the struggle between being fully human and being "a man"? Still, the bottom line is that everyone does this thing called grief in different ways. Judging each other or carrying expectations of a best way to grieve is never fruitful.

Expectations also may get in the way of acknowledging change during special times for your family. Formerly you may have looked forward to holidays, anniversaries, birthdays, and other occasions. Following the death of a loved one, intense anxiety, fear, or pain may cloud your anticipation. What once excited you now produces dread and dismay. The anticipation of such events seems to be the most difficult piece of grieving. But with some simple planning and specific tasks, special days can become less a burden and more a time for reflection:

- Plan ahead. Determine what you need to make these times less stressful. Which supportive and understanding people will you hang out with? Are you most comfortable at home or away? Schedule activities that you want to keep the same this year. Give yourself permission to limit your commitments, and avoid unimportant obligations.

- Communicate your wishes to others. You might wish to call a family meeting to plan the special event. This can be a time of sharing your thoughts and feelings with others and giving your loved ones an opportunity to share their ideas, too. Use this forum to begin delegating specific tasks and traditions that continue to be important for you and your family.

- Acknowledge your limitations. This is a time to be gentle and kind to yourself. Be aware that less is more and simpler is better. Set aside time to be still and to rest. Plan activities that nurture you and others physically, emotionally, and spiritually. Lower your expectations of yourself and others, and embrace this new place in your life.

- Acknowledge your loss and grief. This can be a time to plan a new activity or ritual in memory of your loved one. Hang a special stocking, light a special candle, hang a memorial wreath, or decorate a tree with symbols of your loved one. Know that it is all right to express your thoughts and feelings at this special time of grieving. Nothing can make you or your family sadder, so release your tears and grief.

- Embrace the memories and create new traditions. It is helpful and healing to say the name of the one you love. Share pictures and stories. Laugh and cry. Tell your story in your holiday greetings. Consider a holiday donation with the money you might have spent on your loved one. Some find it helpful to visit the cemetery and place some special object there. Consider adopting a family in need, giving a memorial gift, or extending a special holiday invitation.

- Evaluate your shopping plan. Decide whether shopping in a decorated store or mall will be too difficult. Shop before the explosion of décor and music begins, or consider shopping by mail. Establish your priorities according to your level of energy.

- Accept help from others. Remember that grief demands your attention and requires a great deal of time and energy. Asking others for help may be your greatest gift to them. This provides opportunities for others to become involved and allows you to take time for yourself. Inquire about the support available through your faith community, and be open to the idea of grief support groups or therapy.

Remember that grief is a natural experience that comes into your life because of the love you have given and received. Acknowledge the loss you are experiencing and begin to embrace a new sense of connectedness to the ones you love. You may develop a new sense of hope and a new sense of who you are and what life is truly about. Change is constant in your life, and this becomes more evident during times of loss and grief.

Praise to Early-Waking Grievers

I was sleeping, and being comforted
By a cool breeze, when suddenly a gray dove
From a thicket sang and sobbed with longing
And reminded me of my own passion.
I had been away from my own soul so long,
So late-sleeping, but that dove's crying
Woke me and made me cry.
Praise to all early-waking grievers!

—Adi al-Riga

Needed . . .

A strong person wise enough to allow me to grieve in
the depth of who I am

And strong enough to hear my pain, without turning
away.

Not too close because then you couldn't help me to
see.

Not too objective because then you might not care.

Not too aloof because then you could not hug me.

Not too caring because I'd be tempted to let you live
my life for me.

I need someone who believes that the sun will rise
again

But who does not fear my darkness or my walk through
the night,

Someone who can point out the rocks in my way
without making me a child by carrying me,

Someone who can stand in the thunder and watch the
lightning and believe in a rainbow.

—*Father Joe Mahoney*

6

Healing Concepts

At first, you can delay the stark reality of loss and grief through common coping mechanisms, like blocking your grief. Fighting back your emotions may seem like the right thing to do, so you choose to keep busy and begin to "move on with life." But your expectations of others may launch you into a place you don't seem to belong, adding to your potential for isolation. How do you begin to work through your grief? How do you pay attention to these new thoughts and feelings?

After the deaths of their children, Ken described his and Lorrie's dilemma in this way: "The crisis was over for others, and we were left alone to figure it out! The party was over, and the band packed up and went home."

Life became unfamiliar, and the theme of change was everywhere. Ken eventually was unable to work. His personal grief reactions became more and more complicated, affecting every dimension of his being. And then he learned he would have to seek therapy to remain on paid disability. He received multiple referrals pointing to the Center for Grief, Loss & Transition and so continued his journey—with great reluctance: "What could anyone say or do to relieve our pain? How could anyone understand our loss? They don't know our family. They don't know the joy and plans we had."

As grief-therapy sessions proceeded, Ken's attitude began to change. Therapy became a place where someone would listen and give permission for expression and venting of his different emotions. This intentional way to release some of the pressures of grief became something for him to look forward to. He was able to share his process openly with his wife and begin to accept some of the changes before him. He established new ways of coping. The reality of their new and different life began to surface, bit by bit.

This doesn't mean, of course, that everyone who has a loss must seek therapy. But you need an understanding that you can't do this alone and that your natural instincts about what can help may not be right on. Finding someone to listen to your story again and again may be a challenge.

Remember, suffering alone does not teach. Time does *not* heal all wounds. For healing to begin, intentional grief work is necessary. Developing tools and skills to help you accommodate to your changed world is necessary. So what helps you to begin this healing process?

Here are a few ideas:

1. Companions for the journey. Are you spending enough time with others who truly care about you and who validate your personal grief process? Clergy, friends who "get it," family members who "get it," a grief group, or a grief therapist may be on your list. Do you feel cared for, understood, and validated in your experience?

2. Time for your grief. How much time do you spend each day acknowledging and taking care of yourself? Grief demands your attention. You have not failed and you aren't "going crazy"—you are grieving, which takes time.

3. Permission for expression. Is it okay for you to feel a mix of emotions? Discover different ways to externalize your thoughts and feelings of grief. Talking, crying, and laughing are okay. Loss is the problem, not you.

4. Becoming an expert. Are you curious about this life experience? Pay attention to what grief feels like, how it ebbs and flows, and what helps it to diminish. Gathering information about your loss can reduce anxiety.

5. Naming what is lost and what is not. Have you focused both on what you have lost and on what you have left? Clarifying your multiple losses and recognizing both what is left and what may come can lead to hope.

6. Being kind to yourself. Are you paying attention to yourself? Realize that you can't do this alone. Do what you can and not what others think or say you should do. Promote a sense of calm and healing. It's okay to take a break from your grief.

7. Embracing imperfection. Realize that you don't have all the answers. You will continue to make good and bad choices. When it feels as if you can't make any more decisions, don't.

8. Creating places of sanctuary. Where do you feel safe and free to be real with your grief? Peaceful environments in and out of your home allow you to fulfill your need for peace, quiet, and escape. Find the places that nourish you—you may have some favorites already.

Remember that you won't simply "get over" your grief. Rather, it sits on your shoulder. But if you periodically turn your head and look at it straight on, the honest acknowledgment of your pain will bring relief. Grief is hard work, and it will take as long as it takes. Being still and present in times of despair is a healing approach to this work. Grieving can become a sacred and creative time for you to discover who you are and how you choose to transform your life. Many have discovered that they can hold on to two opposing ideas—grief and hope—at the same time. You can, too.

Pay attention, also, to the concepts that are not healing. This can be a time of discovering what works and what doesn't work for you.

Temporary coping techniques may help at first, then quickly add to your grief. Self-medicating with alcohol or drugs to relieve your pain is just one example. We live in a society that copes with physical pain by taking substances to relieve it. Unfortunately, this may only further complicate your process. Alcohol is a depressant, not a friend to grief. It alters your reality and, in the long run, only makes your grief worse. Become familiar with patterns of alcoholism, compulsive behavior, addictions, and depression in your family history. Loss and grief can easily trigger such predispositions.

This is a time to be gentle with yourself. If you are challenged by self-care concepts, you will be challenged in your grief. See chapter 8 for specific ideas about how to take better care of yourself.

Some people journeying with grief say that "moments of connectedness" comprise one of the most powerful aids to healing. They describe times during which they feel strongly that a loved one is present—a visitation, a dream, a sign or symbol.

Ken described such a visitation from his son Matthew. The experience was so overwhelming that initially he could not share it outside of a therapy session. Ken was spending a fair amount of time in his garage, seeking solace and quiet time. He began to feel his son's presence, then noticed him sitting on a cooler in the rafters. They looked at each other, and Ken began to cry. Matthew looked great. He seemed content, conveying a sense that he was okay and wanted his family to be okay too. The next thing that happened took Ken's breath away. Matthew swooped down and kissed him on the cheek. Then he returned to the rafters and was gone. This visitation was an intense, emotional gift that gave Ken a sense his son was all right and was encouraging him to be all right as well.

Others have described vivid dreams after which they felt a sense of time spent with their loved ones. Some describe events such as lights suddenly turning on or off or coins found in various places in and out of the home. Such events cannot be fully understood or explained, yet they provide healing for those who are open to the phenomenon. Frequent sightings of special birds like cardinals, hummingbirds, and eagles are healing reminders for many.

The Elephant in the Room

There's an elephant in the room.
It is large and squatting, so it is hard to get around.
Yet we squeeze by with "How are you?" and "I'm fine,"
And a thousand other forms of trivial chatter.
We talk about the weather.
We talk about work.
We talk about everything else, except the elephant in the
    room.
There's an elephant in the room.
We all know it is there.
We are thinking about the elephant as we talk together.
It is constantly on our minds.
For, you see, it is a very large elephant.
It has hurt us all.
But we do not talk about the elephant in the room.
Oh, please say his name.
Oh, please say it again.
Oh, please, let's talk about the elephant in the room.
For if we talk about his death, perhaps we could talk
    about his life.
Can I say his name to you and not have you look away?
For if I cannot, then you are leaving me . . .
Alone . . . in a room . . . with an elephant.

—*Terri Kettering*

7

Am I Stuck?

Death is oblivious to age, income, religion, or race. It may come without warning or clear cause. It may follow a long, painful illness, yet it continues to demand your attention. Death brings about many reactions in widely contrasting combinations. No one can tell you how to grieve, or for how long. It is a unique experience for each person.

I am often asked whether a particular grief reaction is normal. What is "normal"? Perhaps the best, general understanding is that what you are experiencing is where you need to be. Clients often refer to life before the loss and after the loss. What develops is a "new normal."

I once worked with a client, Jack, who had lost his wife to chronic depression and ultimately to suicide. He was preoccupied and restless at the beginning of a session, nearing the end of many months of therapy. He was concerned about and questioned whether he was stuck in his grieving. A friend had told Jack that he should be dating, moving on with his life, that Jack needed a wife, and his children needed a mother. In truth, Jack had been functioning very well, and he was pleased with the grief work and progress he had achieved.

This well-intentioned friend created new concerns for Jack, who already was facing the challenges of a young widower. Loneliness, isolation, and adjusting to the demands of single parenthood were daily concerns. Questioning whether he was stuck in his grief (that is, becoming depressed) exacerbated his already complicated responses and life adjustments. But Jack, by virtue of his ability to pay attention to his own reactions to grief and to question his progress, is a clear example of someone actively grieving as opposed to being stuck. Taking the time to listen to others, especially to yourself, helps ward off isolation and withdrawal into a smaller world.

Grieving may become more complicated when the pain of your loss is extreme or when it is simply too large to embrace. You may have been dealt more than you can handle—more than anyone could handle. Grief may quickly become depression, a distortion of reality or a battle towards avoidance. This twist may occur for any one of many different reasons.

The relationship you had with a person who is gone affects the way you respond to your loss. Your loss may prompt a time of self-reflection, as you question what you meant to your loved one or question any aspect of the relationship you had. A strained relationship means a more complicated grief process. Guilt and shame may hinder your entry into a healthy place to begin your grief. Intense feelings of rage or resentment may become the focus of your day. You may feel judged by others, or you may feel undeserving of support. You may need permission (many do) to share these thoughts and fears with another.

I am periodically challenged by stories of guilt and shame. Cindy and Larry were reeling after their daughter completed a suicide in their home. Larry had returned home from work and found his beloved child in her room. After finding the hidden key, she had taken his gun from a locked safe.

The horror of the reality was almost too much for Larry to bear. And on top of that, he had to tell his wife of the tragedy. His attempts to protect and soften the experience proved futile. Cindy needed to know what happened and what her husband had seen.

Life as Larry and Cindy knew it forever changed that day. Their family now consisted of a mother and a father with no living child. For many months they asked: "Why did this happen to our family? Why didn't we do something to prevent it? Why weren't we better parents? Why weren't we better informed about depression? Why did I say that to her? Why didn't I say this to her?"

What-ifs and second-guessing became all consuming. Larry and Cindy hadn't signed up for such an event, and they were lost in their pain. They were left with the new reality that they were not the parents of a living child who needed them. Self-inflicted responsibility for their child's death became their reality.

This couple's therapy eventually turned into sessions for Cindy alone. Larry's pain became isolating, which diminished their openness to sharing their responses and glimpses of the world. Larry continues to spend time alone, and he drinks more than he used to, while Cindy has remained intentional in her grief work. She has brought new meaning into her life through her volunteer work with children and her journaling. And as if she hadn't enough to work through in her life, she has decided to face her fear of flying and is now traveling a great deal more than she did before.

The manner of death may launch those left behind into an unknown, challenging place. A traumatic death from homicide, suicide, or an accident may create a shift in your sense of what is real and safe. Unexpected loss may jolt you out of the sense of who you are. The death of a child takes away your envisioned future. Multiple losses signal the potential for just too much to handle. Intense feelings of blame or revenge overshadow common ways of coping. Sadness may turn you to depression or turn you away from others.

Traumatic loss may complicate your grief. The losses resulting from a death can be staggering. Adjustment and reevaluation of what remains in your life may be too painful to attempt at any given point. Your grief may interfere with your ability to participate fully. A lack of energy and the will to live may become familiar.

These types of losses and complicated responses require special attention. Do not assume that you must overcome complicated grief by yourself. Help from a professional can enable you to gather the tools and skills that promote healing. You need a place of safety and a sense of support. Healing requires an honest understanding of responses and validation of your new life reality. You must be allowed to tell your story without judgment or ridicule.

You may complicate your grief even more by trying to avoid emotionally what has happened to you. Inability to fully acknowledge your loss or to feel and express your resulting deep feelings ultimately impedes your healthy grief experience.

Perhaps you've struggled all your life to tolerate pain or show your feelings. Perhaps you didn't even know it. If that is the case, shedding that pattern will be a challenge. A sense of helplessness or lack of control may launch you into a place of avoidance. Try to identify the triggers—persons, places, situations—of your feelings. And don't avoid them. Sidestepping reminders of your loss may provide a false sense of survival. You may just be postponing the inevitable. Grief will not be denied—it will only sit and wait for you.

Being open to the reality of your loss and grief and being willing to acknowledge your responses, thoughts, and feelings allow healing and help to resolve complication.

When you worry about the progression of your grief and question what is normal and what is not, try to see your responses in context. Is there a reason for feeling the way you do? Clearly recognizing your losses, being aware of more ambiguous losses, points the way to the fact that you are dealing with grief. Shift some of your attention from your losses, to how you are dealing with them.

If you feel stuck in a depressed state with little or no change, take it as a sign of complication. Chapter 2 lists some common reactions to grief. Look at these as normal, natural responses to loss events. In contrast, the following is a list of potentially complicated responses:

- Persistent, negative thoughts and feelings
- Marked changes in sleeping patterns/sleep disorder
- Marked changes in eating patterns/eating disorder
- Self-harming or risky behavior
- Increased isolation and despair
- Substance abuse
- Suicidal thoughts
- Homicidal thoughts
- Feeling depressed

There are significant differences between grief and depression. Grieving has been described at length in earlier chapters. It is characterized by a preoccupation with a loss and by ever-changing shifts in mood. With depression, there is not always an identifiable loss, and the focus tends to be negative perceptions of self. Depression usually causes an emotionally fixed state of being, characterized by feelings of despair, withdrawal, and being stuck. Professional consultation with a qualified therapist and physician is necessary for a diagnosis of your psychological state. Address signs of clinical depression specifically, with a psychiatrist who can best discuss medication options along with talk therapy.

I have often seen clients beginning to fit the criteria listed above during the course of therapy. For Jane, therapy was coming to a close—she reported functioning well and returning to work after the sudden death of her husband. She had begun to talk about her plans for the future, including dating and returning to school.

But one afternoon I received a message that Jane was admitting herself to the hospital. She had been able to discern that her grief was becoming complicated by chronic, physical pain; she was becoming hopeless. She experienced feelings of isolation and a sense that she had no real future. These feelings began to concern her more when thoughts of suicide seemed to provide an option.

Jane was able to call a helpful friend, her physician, and me, her therapist. She was able to create a safe environment and become open to the professional help she clearly needed. She was able to recognize what could help her out of her despair. She knew she had to talk to as many helpful people as possible and avoid those who might not be helpful in a time of crisis. The hospital staff, her physician, and her friends were supportive. She stated that having a good therapist helped her turn the corner and choose life.

Listening to yourself and others is critical during such times—you may benefit from the help of a physician and therapist. Err on the side of getting more help than you may need. Asking for help does not mean something is wrong with you. It means that you are smart enough to know that you do not have the tools to point you in the right direction.

The natural tendency is to withdraw, but that is the least helpful action. Everyone in grief needs support from others and gentleness from within.

Our society places great importance on how we look and not on how we feel. We tend to judge books by their covers and not by what is inside. We seem to be better at scheduling hair, dental, and nail appointments than we are at paying attention to our thoughts, feelings, and mental health. Take note of that and be good to yourself. Intentional self-care makes all the difference. Start by getting the help you need. But, you ask, "How do I know I need help at all?"

- Your grief doesn't change.
- Your grief interferes with your ability to function.
- You function as though nothing has changed.
- Your self-esteem remains at a low level.
- Guilt and/or anger overwhelm you.
- You withdraw from others.
- You frequently think about hurting yourself or someone else.
- You have lost your will to live.
- You cope with your loss through addictive behaviors.
- You believe you are depressed.
- You have developed destructive and/or risk-taking behaviors.
- You have recurring flashbacks.

At the back of this book is a list of resources for your use. Finding an experienced therapist in your area may prove your most helpful move towards healing. This may not always feel necessary, but you can count on being overwhelmed as the days come and go. Have someone you trust on board for those difficult times.

Therapy groups may also be available in your area. These groups of individuals experiencing similar losses are led by experienced therapists. Support groups are another forum for you to consider. You may find these groups, facilitated by volunteers, through church coalitions or hospitals. Contacting a church in your area is a good place to start.

Meditations of the Heart

I share with you the agony of your grief,
The anguish of your heart finds echo in my own.
I know I cannot enter all you feel
Nor bear with you the burden of your pain.
I can but offer what my love does give,
The strength of caring,
The warmth of one who seeks to understand
The silent storm-swept barrenness of so great a loss.
This I do in quiet ways,
That on your lonely path
You may not walk alone.

—Howard Thurman

This life is not concerned with health but with
   healing.
This life is not about our being but our becoming.
This life is not about rest but about exercise.
We are not yet what we shall be, but we are growing
   toward it.
The process is not yet finished but it is going on.
This is not the end but it's the road.

—*Martin Luther*

8

Creating Self-Care

In a culture overcome by demands, expectations, and stress, paying attention to and being intentional about your grief process may be difficult. Some mourners believe it can wait, while others try to avoid it. Grief will not be pushed aside or denied. Trying to postpone your grieving merely delays your healing. And as your grief waits, it festers, growing in intensity, creating more misery in the interim. It can rob you of reality, energy, and your ability to forgive. It may rip away your sense of self and your desire to live.

Ken and Lorrie were living in this place of despair. Perhaps their greatest piece of self-care was putting into words their experience of hopelessness. Ken shared great insight through this process in a gathering for supporters of the Center for Grief, Loss & Transition. The following excerpts from his sharings tell the story:

Ken and Lorrie received therapeutic referrals from the hospital chaplain, their pastor, and physicians. Ken began his journey as a reluctant participant. Again, he said, "What could anyone say or do to relieve our pain? How could anyone understand our loss? They didn't know our family. They didn't know the joy. They didn't know our plans."

But as Ken and Lorrie began their therapy sessions, his attitude began to change. Therapy became a place where someone listened and "gave us permission to express and vent all the different emotions we were feeling." It soon became something they needed and looked forward to. They found different ways to express feelings: journal writing, letter writing, and reading. As they learned to express anger, sadness, and disappointment, things began to change. They began to smile and to laugh again and to understand that it was all right to do so. They were able to experience joy in small doses. They began to talk about their future.

This transformation took time, but given their initial hopelessness, the change was amazing. This too was a life-changing experience.

Letting go of some of the things they had lost and embracing a new life were crucial to Ken and Lorrie and their family.

Their individual, couple, and group therapy sessions proved invaluable. Ken felt they had learned so many things over the three years since the fatal accident. They could speak of some of these things, but there seemed to be no words for others. They often used a few main themes to speak of their experience and of what they had learned, ideas for living the rest of their lives:

- Be kind to yourself.
- You can't do it alone.
- Do what you can and not what others think you should do.
- Know what it feels like and what it is that you need to do.

Ken had been the most reluctant to participate in group therapy— it's one thing to express yourself in a setting with family and a therapist; it's another to show yourself to a group of strangers. "What an amazing experience this was!" he said. "You get to meet wonderful people and share their stories. The value in hearing others' stories and sharing yours is indescribable. You begin to realize that you are not alone and that you are not crazy for feeling some of the things you are feeling. You get to see nothing but genuine human emotion. Bonds form quickly and you even gain some lasting friendships. Bad things truly do happen to good people. You learn that all stories are not sensational and not all of them make the news, but the pain that people experience is the same. It is incredible to share your story with others who do not yet see any hope and watch them gradually look to the future."

Ken and Lorrie learned that their son was experiencing the same range of emotions they did. He was able to learn to express his anger, loneliness, and sadness. He now keeps a journal, writes stories and songs, and does not hesitate to talk about his brother and sister. He tells you when he is sad and gives a hug when he thinks someone needs one. Mike has made a miraculous recovery from the accident. Although left with some disabilities due to his injuries, he will lead a full life. He is courageous, an inspiration. Despite their sad story, Ken and Lorrie wish to leave only their message of hope—hope that others may receive the help that they did to heal and renew their lives.

The challenge before you is to simplify your life, acknowledge your losses, and make space for your grief. Spend a little time exploring your life realities. It will help you reprioritize what you do and what you want to be.

Most people are not very good at taking care of themselves. Being available to others and putting your own needs aside may feel more natural to you. But whatever your situation, grief will demand that you take care of yourself. If you know that taking care of yourself has been a lifelong challenge, this is the time to stop and pay attention to your life.

- How much time do I spend each day acknowledging and taking care of myself?

- Do I spend time with others who truly care about me and help me in my process?

- Am I able to delegate certain tasks and responsibilities to others?

- Do I take time for myself to promote a sense of calm, healing, and growth?

During difficult times it is critical that we pay attention to what seems to help us feel better, to what allows us to better cope with the day. What do you do to balance the five dimensions of self: physical, emotional, spiritual, behavioral, and cognitive?

Sharing and gathering ideas with others is a good way to start. Schedule some time for yourself to treat yourself well and do what you love. Make your own self-care list, perhaps including some of the following:

- Listening to or playing music
- Writing/journaling
- Creative activities: scrapbooking, drawing, knitting, gardening
- Reading
- Therapeutic environments: individual/family therapy, grief group, spiritual direction, place of worship
- Spiritual journey/retreat
- Meditation
- Getting enough sleep
- Individual/family rituals: acknowledging anniversaries, birthdays, and holidays
- Quiet times
- Volunteer time
- Establishing a memorial fund/scholarship

Your Self-Care Plan

Simplify and seek support
Establish a place of sanctuary
Let go and embrace a sense of hope
Feel your feelings

Challenge yourself and celebrate with play and humor
Ask for help and acknowledge your reality
Rest and relax
Exercise and eat well

PLUS, make a list of five people who are helpful to you and five activities that make you feel better. Plan your life including them.

No one can tell you how or how not to grieve. Allow yourself the time and patience your grief demands. This grieving journey is like seasonal change in your soul—fall, winter, spring, and a renewed hope and courage in the summer of your life.

The Journey

One day you finally knew
what you had to do, and began,
though the voices around you
kept shouting
their bad advice—
though the whole house
began to tremble
and you felt the old tug
at your ankles.
"Mend my life!"
each voice cried.
But you didn't stop.
You knew what you had to do,
though the wind pried
with its stiff fingers
at the very foundations,
though their melancholy
was terrible.
It was already late
enough, and a wild night,
and the road full of fallen
branches and stones.

—Thomas M. Ellis—

But little by little,
as you left their voices behind,
the stars began to burn
through the sheets of clouds,
and there was a new voice
which you slowly
recognized as your own,
that kept you company
as you strode deeper and deeper
into the world,
determined to do
the only thing you could do—
determined to save
the only life you could save.

—Mary Oliver

Resources

Where to Go for Help

American Cancer Society
   Toll-free: 800-ACS-2345
   www.cancer.org

American Red Cross National Headquarters
   2025 E Street, NW
   Washington, DC 20006
   Phone: 202-303-4498
   www.redcross.org

American SIDS Institute
Works to prevent sudden infant death and to promote infant health through programs of research, clinical services, education, and family support.
509 Augusta Drive
Marietta, GA 30067
Toll-free: 800-232-SIDS
www.sids.org

The Association for Death Education and Counseling (ADEC)
Offers numerous educational opportunities through its annual conference, courses, and workshops, its certification program, and its acclaimed newsletter, *The Forum.*
60 Revere Drive, Suite 500
Northbrook, IL 60062 USA
Phone: 847-509-0403
www.adec.org

Center for Grief, Loss & Transition
Provides therapy and education in the areas of complicated grief, trauma, and life transitions.
1133 Grand Avenue
St. Paul, MN 55105
Phone: 651-641-0177
www.griefloss.org

The Compassionate Friends, Inc.
Assists families towards the positive resolution of grief following the death of a child of any age and provides information to help others be supportive.
    P. O. Box 3696
    Oak Brook, IL 60522-3696
    Toll-free: 877-969-0010
    www.compassionatefriends.org

The National Funeral Directors Association (NFDA)
Provides advocacy, education, information, products, programs, and services to help members enhance the quality of service to families.
    13625 Bishop's Drive
    Brookfield, WI 53005
    Toll-free: 800-228-6332
    www.nfda.org

The National Hospice and Palliative Care Organization (NHPCO)
The largest nonprofit membership organization representing hospice and palliative care programs and professionals in the United States, working to improve end-of-life care and expand access to hospice care so as to enhance the quality of life for people who are dying and for their loved ones.
    1700 Diagonal Road, Suite 625
    Alexandria, VA 22314
    Phone: 703-837-1500
    www.nhpco.org

Parents of Murdered Children, Inc.
A national organization for the families and friends of those who have died by violence, provides emotional support, education, prevention, advocacy, and awareness.

    100 East Eighth Street, Suite B-41
    Cincinnati, OH 45202
    Toll-free: 888-818-POMC
    www.pomc.com

Suicide Awareness Voices of Education (SAVE)
Works to prevent suicide through public awareness and education, to eliminate stigma, and to serve as a resource to those touched by suicide.

    9001 East Bloomington Freeway
    Suite #150
    Bloomington, MN 55420
    Phone: 952-946-7998
    www.save.org

And You Might Want to Read . . .

Grief and Loss

Amatuzio, Janis. *Forever Ours.* Novato, CA: New World Library, 2004. Real stories of immortality and living from a forensic pathologist.

Boss, Pauline. *Ambiguous Loss.* Cambridge, MA: Harvard University Press, 2000. Learning to live with unresolved grief.

Bozarth, Alla. *A Journey through Grief.* Minneapolis: Compcare, 1990. Short, gentle book on the grief process.

———. *Life Is Good-bye, Life Is Hello: Grieving Well through All Kinds of Losses.* Minneapolis: Compcare, 1982. A hopeful message for all losses.

Brener, Anne. *Mourning and Mitzvah.* Woodstock, MA: Jewish Lights, 1993. A guided journal for walking the mourner's path.

Caine, Lynn. *Being a Widow.* New York: Penguin, 1989. Self-help for widows.

Diets, Bob. *Life after Loss.* Tucson: Fisher Books, 1992. A personal guide dealing with death, divorce, job change, and relocation.

Duerk, Judith. *Circle of Stones.* Maui: Inner Ocean, 1999. A woman's journey to herself.

Edelmann, Hope. *Motherless Daughters: The Legacy of Loss.* New York: Dell, 1995.

Elison, Jennifer, and Chris McGonigle. *Liberating Losses: When Death Brings Relief.* Cambridge, MA: Da Capo Lifelong (Perseus), 2003.

Ericsson, Stephanie. *Companion through the Darkness: Inner Dialogues on Grief.* New York: HarperCollins, 1993. A personal, poetic guide for significant others.

Fischer, Bruce, and Robert Alberti. *Rebuilding: When Your Relationship Ends.* Atascadero, CA: Impact, 2000. Divorce recovery.

Fitzgerald, Helen. *The Grieving Child: A Parent's Guide to Understanding Children.* New York: Simon & Schuster, 1992.

Grollman, Earl. *Talking about Death: A Dialogue between Parent and Child.* New York: Macmillan, 1993.

Irish, Donald, Kathleen Lundquist, and Vivian Jenkins Nelson. *Ethnic Variations in Dying, Death and Grief: Diversity in Universality.* Washington, DC: Taylor & Francis, 1993.

Jarratt, Claudia Jewett. *Helping Children Cope with Separation and Loss.* Boston: Harvard Common, 1994. Aimed at any adult helping a grieving child, this book discusses the various "stages" of mourning and the type of behavior shown by children throughout the grieving process. Outlines techniques to help children through their grief.

Klass, Dennis, Phyllis Silverman, and Steven Nickman. *Continuing Bonds: New Understandings of Grief.* London: Taylor & Francis, 1996.

Kushner, Rabbi Harold. *How Good Do We Have to Be? A New Understanding of Guilt and Forgiveness.* Boston: Little, Brown, 1996. Embraces imperfections and teaches how to accept ourselves.

———. *When Bad Things Happen to Good People.* Boston: Beacon, 1981. Rabbi Kushner reflects upon the "why" of suffering following his son's illness and death.

LeVang, Elizabeth, and Sherokee Ilse. *Remembering with Love.* Minneapolis: Deaconess, 1992. Short messages of compassion, comfort, and guidance for those grieving the death of someone they love.

Lewis, C. S. *A Grief Observed.* San Francisco: Harper, 1961. Renowned author's journal following his wife's death. This book is an honest reflection on the fundamental issues of life, death, and faith. Summons those who grieve to honest mourning and courageous hope.

Lightner, Candy, and Nancy Hathaway. *Giving Sorrow Words.* New York: Warner, 1990. By a mother (founder of MADD) whose daughter died in an accident.

Martin, Terry, and Kenneth Doka. *Men Don't Cry, Women Do: Transcending Gender Stereotypes of Grief.* Philadelphia: Brunner Mazel, 2000. On different grieving styles.

Menten, Ted. *After Goodbye.* Philadelphia: Running Press, 1994. Hopeful book of stories about love and loss.

O'Fallon, Ann, and Margaret Vaillancourt. *Kiss Me Goodnight.* Minneapolis: Syren, 2005. Stories of women who were children when their mothers died.

Price, Eugenia. *Getting through the Night.* New York: Dial, 1982. Inspirational, Christian perspective on grief.

Rando, Therese. *How to Go on Living When Someone You Love Dies.* New York: Bantam, 1991.

Remen, Rachel. *Kitchen Table Wisdom.* Denver: Trade, 2001.

Rothman, Juliet. *The Bereaved Parents' Survival Guide*. New York: Continuum, 1997. For parents following the death of a child.

Schneider, John. *Finding My Way*. Colfax, WI: Seasons, 1994. Educational text on transformative grief.

Tatelbaum, Judy. *The Courage to Grieve*. New York: Harper & Row, 1980. General grief book about hope and self-care.

Ziegler, David. *Raising Children Who Refuse to Be Raised*. Phoenix: Acacia, 2000. How to help challenging children who struggle against your every effort as a parent or therapist to help them succeed in the world.

Trauma

Bolton, Iris, and Curtis Mitchell. *My Son, My Son*. Atlanta: Bolton, 1983. For parents who have lost a child to suicide.

Fine, Carla, and David Kessler. *No Time to Say Goodbye: Surviving the Suicide of a Loved One*. New York: Broadway, 2000.

Herman, Judith. *Trauma and Recovery*. Maryland: Basic, 1992

Lord, Janice. *No Time for Goodbyes*. Ventura, CA: Pathfinder, 1990. Coping with sadness, anger, trauma, and injustice after a tragic death.

Matsakis, Aphrodite. *I Can't Get over It*. Oakland, CA: New Harbinger, 1996. A self-help book for those who have experienced trauma.

———. *Trust after Trauma: A Guide to Relationships*. Oakland, CA: New Harbinger, 1998. For survivors and those who love them.

Najavits, Lisa. *Seeking Safety: A Treatment Manual for PTSD and Substance Abuse.* New York: Guilford: 2001.

Robinson, Rita. *Survivors of Suicide.* Franklin Lakes, NJ: Franklin Lakes Press, 2001.

Rosenbloom, Dena. *Life after Trauma: A Workbook for Healing.* New York: Guilford, 1999.

Thich Nhat Hanh. *Taming the Tiger Within.* Rochester, NY: Berkeley, 2004. Meditations on transforming difficult emotions.

Wrobleski, Adina. *Suicide of a Child.* Omaha: Centering Corporation, 1984.

———. *Suicide Survivors: A Guide for Those Left Behind.* Minneapolis: Afterwords, 1994.

Miscarriage

Ilse, Sherokee, and Linda Burns. *Empty Arms.* Maple Plain, MN: Wintergreen, 2002. Miscarriage, stillbirth, and infant loss.

———. *Miscarriage: A Shattered Dream.* Maple Plain, MN: Wintergreen, 2002. A comprehensive and insightful perspective on possible causes, medical terminology, and choices and decisions for families experiencing a miscarriage. Examines the emotional aspects of miscarriage, offers coping suggestions, and discusses choices for the future. Includes resources and bibliography.

Vredevelt, Pam. *Two Empty Arms.* New York: Questar, 1995. Emotional support for those who have suffered miscarriage or stillbirth.

Terminal Illness

Albom, Mitch. *Tuesdays with Morrie*. New York: Bantam Doubleday, 1997. A beautiful tribute to aging.

Broyard, Anatole. *Intoxicated by My Illness and Other Writings on Life and Death*. New York: Ballantine, 1992. The author's personal response to his illness.

Choprak, Deepak. *Quantum Healing: Exploring the Frontiers of Mind/Body Medicine*. Louisville: Crown, 1991.

Kübler-Ross, Elisabeth. *The Wheel of Life: A Memoir of Living and Dying*. New York: Touchstone (Simon & Schuster), 1998.

Kübler-Ross, Elisabeth, and David Kessler. *Life Lessons*. New York: Touchstone, 2002.

Levine, Stephen. *Meetings at the Edge*. New York: Doubleday, 1980.

Rinpoche, Sogyal. *Tibetan Book on Living and Dying*. San Francisco: HarperCollins, 2002. A lucid and inspiring introduction to the practice of meditation, karma, compassionate love, and care for the dying.

For Children and the Young at Heart

Bianco, Marjorie. *The Velveteen Rabbit*. New York: Doubleday, 2005. Classic tale of transformation and love.

Buscaglia, Leo. *The Fall of Freddie the Leaf*. New York: Holt, Rinehart & Winston, 1982. Inspiring allegory illustrating the delicate balance between life and death.

Curtis, Jamie Lee. *Today I Feel Silly and Other Moods That Make My Day.* New York: HarperCollins, 1998. Helps children explore and identify their ever-changing moods.

———. *Where Do Balloons Go? An Uplifting Mystery.* New York: HarperCollins, 1998.

dePaola, Tomie. *Nana Upstairs & Nana Downstairs.* New York: G. P. Putnam's Sons, 1973.

Dokas, Dara. *Remembering MaMa.* Minneapolis: Augsburg, 2002. Illustrates the gift of memories.

Hanson, Warren. *The Next Place.* Minneapolis: Waldman House, 1997. An inspirational journey of hope and wonder, to a place where earthly hurts are left behind.

Harris, Robie. *Goodbye Mousie.* New York: Simon & Schuster Children's Books, 2003.

Parr, Todd. *It's Okay to Be Different.* New York: Little, Brown, 2001. Simple, playful celebration of diversity.

Payne, Lauren Murphy. *Just Because I Am: A Child's Book of Affirmation.* Minneapolis: Free Spirit, 1994. Excellent introduction to self-esteem.

Puttock, Simon, and Allison Bartlett. *A Story for Hippo.* New York: Scholastic, 2001. Reassuring answers to questions on grief for very young children.

Schwiebert, Pat, and Chuck Deklyen. *Tear Soup.* Portland, OR: Grief Watch, 2001. Good for all ages.

Sheppard, Caroline. *Brave Bart.* Grosse Pointe Woods, MI: Institute for Trauma and Loss in Children, 1998. A story for traumatized and grieving children.

Shriver, Maria. *What's Heaven?* New York: Golden Books, 1999.

Seuss, Dr. *My Many Colored Days.* New York: Alfred Knopf, 1996. Explains feelings and moods using colors.

———. *Oh, the Places You'll Go.* New York: Random House, 1990. Classic for any age.

Varley, Susan. *Badger's Parting Gifts.* New York: Lothrop, Lee & Shepard, 1984. A tale of woodland animals learning to accept their friend Badger's death.

—Notes—

—Notes—

—Notes—

About the Author

Thomas M. Ellis is a licensed marriage and family therapist and the executive director of the Center for Grief, Loss & Transition, based in Saint Paul. He has worked in the area of grief and loss since 1983, focusing especially on families and trauma. Ellis is also an educator and provider of community training, clinical supervision, organizational consultation, and professional speaking on topics related to grief and loss. He owned and operated a funeral home for 20 years in Hastings, Minnesota, where he lives with his wife and two daughters.

To order additional copies of *This Thing Called Grief*

Web: www.itascabooks.com

Phone: 1-800-901-3480

Fax: Copy and fill out the form below with credit card information.
Fax to 763-398-0198.

Mail: Copy and fill out the form below. Mail with check or credit card information to:

Syren Book Company, 5120 Cedar Lake Road, Minneapolis, MN 55416

Order Form

Copies	Title / Author	Price	Totals
	This Thing Called Grief / **Thomas M. Ellis**	$14.95	$
	Subtotal		$
	7% sales tax (MN only)		$
	Shipping and handling, first copy		$ 4.00
	Shipping and handling, ___ add'l copies @$1.00 ea.		$
	TOTAL TO REMIT		$

Payment Information:

__ Check Enclosed __ Visa/MasterCard		
Card number:	Expiration date:	
Name on card:		
Billing address:		
City:	State:	Zip:
Signature:	Date:	

Shipping Information:

__ Same as billing address __ Other (enter below)		
Name:		
Address:		
City:	State:	Zip: